weird but true!

FOOD

NATIONAL GEOGRAPHIC KiDS

weird but true!

FOOD

300 bite-size facts about incredible edibles!

WASHINGTON, D.C.

Visit us online:
Kids: kids.nationalgeographic.com
Parents: nationalgeographic.com/books
Librarians and teachers: ngchildrensbooks.org

For information about special discounts for bulk purchases, please contact National Geographic Books Special Sales: ngspecsales@ngs.org

For rights or permissions inquiries, please contact National Geographic Books Subsidiary Rights: ngbookrights@ngs.org

Paperback ISBN: 978-1-4263-1871-9
Reinforced Library Binding
ISBN: 978-1-4263-1872-6

Printed in China
15/PPS/1

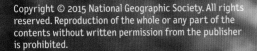

CALL ME SUPERCRAB!

A COCONUT CRAB'S PINCERS ARE STRONG ENOUGH TO CRACK OPEN COCONUT SHELLS.

EATING ICE CREAM MAKES YOUR BODY TEMPERATURE **RISE.**

CREAMY NUTELLA SPREAD WAS FIRST SOLD AS A HARD LOAF.

WITH THE **"TORTILLA BABY,"** YOU CAN DRESS AN INFANT UP TO LOOK LIKE A BURRITO!

6

LIME + KUMQUAT = LIMEQUAT

Cranberries get their name from their **flowers,** which resemble the head and neck of a **crane.**

EATING GARLIC CAN HELP FIGHT A COLD.

REFRIED BEANS ARE FRIED ONLY **ONCE.**

According to a recent study, **Americans crave cheese** more than any other food.

Sliced **grapes** catch **fire** when **cooked** in a **microwave.**

DON'T TRY THIS AT HOME!

Sannakji,
a traditional Korean dish, features
octopus
cut into pieces and served while the tentacles are still
squirming.

Tomatoes are related to deadly nightshade, a very poisonous plant.

3-D PRINTERS may soon be used to make astronauts' **meals** in space.

Listening to high-pitched **music notes** makes food **taste sweeter.**

One year during **prom** season, KFC sold **corsages** made of flowers and fried chicken.

ACTUAL VIDEO!

A BAND SENT A PIECE OF PIZZA INTO **SPACE** AS PART OF A **MUSIC VIDEO.**

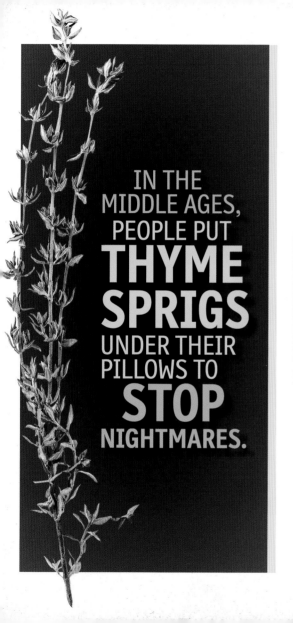

IN THE MIDDLE AGES, PEOPLE PUT **THYME SPRIGS** UNDER THEIR PILLOWS TO **STOP** NIGHTMARES.

Mayonnaise can be used to polish piano keys.

CHERPUMPLE=

a cherry,
a pumpkin, and
an apple pie
stuffed inside a
three-layer cake

Rice Krispies ARE CALLED Rice Bubbles IN AUSTRALIA.

APRICOTS WERE ONCE KNOWN AS GOLDEN APPLES.

19

MYCOPHOBIA:
FEAR OF MUSHROOMS

WHO, ME?!

Zucchinis
can grow as long as three baseball bats lined up end to end.

EVERY DAY, MORE THAN 70 MILLION CUSTOMERS IN OVER 100 COUNTRIES EAT AT A McDONALD'S.

IT TAKES ABOUT

25

TOMATOES

TO MAKE ONE
14-OUNCE (.4 KG) BOTTLE
OF KETCHUP.

Black pudding is a British sausage — made of oatmeal and pig's blood.

24

COFFEE
WAS THE
FIRST FOOD
TO BE
FREEZE-DRIED.

"chyme"
is the word for partially digested food in your stomach.

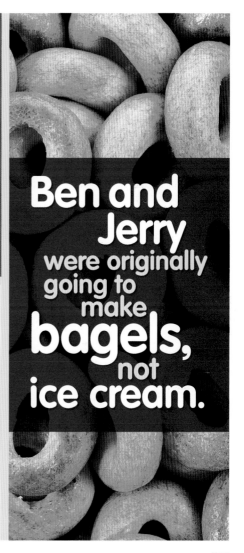

Ben and Jerry were originally going to make bagels, not ice cream.

THE WORLD'S LARGEST CABBAGE WEIGHED AS MUCH AS A ST. BERNARD.

LANGUE DE CHAT, THE NAME OF A LONG, **THIN COOKIE,** MEANS "CAT TONGUE" IN FRENCH.

In the **1960s,** you could buy celery-flavored **Jell-O.**

WORCESTERSHIRE **SAUCE** IS MADE FROM VINEGAR-SOAKED ANCHOVIES.

FARMERS IN OAXACA, **MEXICO,** CELEBRATE THE **NIGHT OF THE RADISHES** ON **DECEMBER 23** BY CARVING **RADISHES** IN THE SHAPE OF **PEOPLE AND FOLK LEGENDS.**

With a price tag of **$1,000,** the world's most expensive *cupcake* contains 23 carats of edible gold.

CIBERO IS AN ITALIAN DISH MADE WITH **COCKSCOMBS,** THE FLESHY RED GROWTH ON TOP OF **CHICKENS' HEADS.**

TURNIPS CAN WEIGH NEARLY AS MUCH AS AN EIGHT-YEAR-OLD KID.

ORIGINAL **RECIPES** FOR **POUND CAKES** CALLED FOR A **POUND** EACH OF (.45 kg) **BUTTER, EGGS, SUGAR,** AND **FLOUR.**

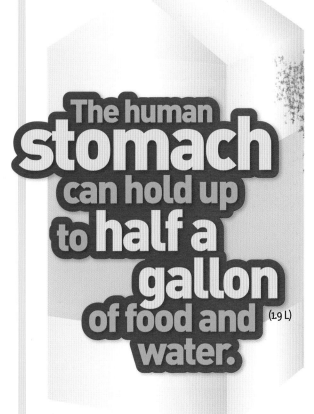

The human **stomach** can hold up to **half a gallon** of food and (1.9 L) water.

Classic scary movie star
Vincent Price
also wrote his own
cookbook.

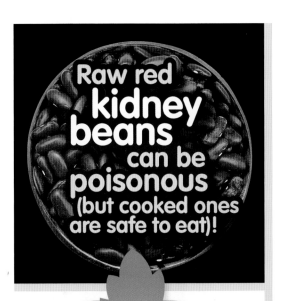

Raw red **kidney beans** can be **poisonous** (but cooked ones are safe to eat)!

Scientists have created a **dairy-free,** plant-based **ice cream.**

USAIN BOLT, *THE WORLD'S FASTEST MAN,* RUNS THE 100-METER DASH AS FAST AS **KETCHUP SQUIRTS** OUT OF A **BOTTLE.**

33

YOUR TASTE BUDS LAST ABOUT 10 DAYS;

THEN YOU GROW
NEW ONES.

ICEBERG LETTUCE IS ALSO CALLED CRISPHEAD.

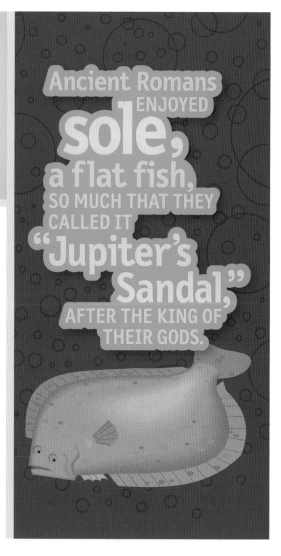

Ancient Romans ENJOYED sole, a flat fish, SO MUCH THAT THEY CALLED IT "Jupiter's Sandal," AFTER THE KING OF THEIR GODS.

Next to oil, coffee is the most valuable commodity in the world.

36

ASTRONAUTS NEIL ARMSTRONG AND BUZZ ALDRIN ATE **HAM-SALAD SANDWICHES** AFTER LANDING ON THE MOON.

President Andrew Jackson kept a **MILK COW** on the White House lawn.

CROISSANT + BAGEL = **CROGEL**

OLiVES ARE
TECHNICALLY A
FRUiT.

Smelling the herb **rosemary** can improve your memory.

The shells of **cashew nuts** can give people an itchy rash.

Edible tattoos may soon be used to mark fruit in grocery stores, instead of stickers.

GALA APPLE

42

SOME 70,000 GALLONS OF BORSCHT— (264,979 L) **A COLD BEET SOUP—WAS SERVED AT THE 2014 OLYMPIC GAMES IN RUSSIA.**

THE CUPUAÇU FRUIT SMELLS LIKE CHOCOLATE AND PINEAPPLE.

During World War II, when food was in short supply, people ate "mock bananas" made from boiled turnips, sugar, and banana flavoring.

AT A RESTAURANT IN TAIWAN, THE TABLES, CHAIRS, DISHES, AND DECORATIONS ARE MADE OF CARDBOARD!

Ancient Romans ate **strawberries** *to cure bad breath.*

The **Carolina Reaper** is the world's **hottest** chili pepper.

45

ABOUT
26 TONS (23.6 mT) OF
GLOWING HOLLOW TURNIPS
ILLUMINATE RICHTERSWIL, **SWITZERLAND'S**
ANNUAL **TURNIP FESTIVAL.**

Hot dogs encased in french fries are a popular street food in South Korea.

Washing your clothes with a teaspoon of **black pepper** keeps colors from fading.

CASU MARZU, A TYPE OF **CHEESE** INFESTED WITH *LIVE, WRIGGLING MAGGOTS,* IS CONSIDERED A DELICACY IN *ITALY.*

THE 100 PLEATS ON A CHEF'S HAT ARE SAID TO REPRESENT ALL THE WAYS YOU CAN COOK AN EGG.

An early version of **Kool-Aid** was called **Fruit Smack.**

AT A SUMMER FESTIVAL IN BARNESVILLE, MINNESOTA, U.S.A., WRESTLERS COMPETE IN A RING FILLED WITH MASHED POTATOES.

YOU CAN START A CAMPFIRE USING AN ORANGE.

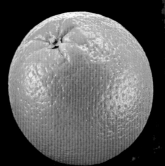

Breakfast waffles inspired the co-founder of **Nike** to put a bumpy **tread** on **running shoes.**

IN GREENLAND, A TRADITIONAL CHRISTMAS FOOD IS MUKTUK— RAW **WHALE SKIN AND BLUBBER.**

THE CHINESE WORD FOR CHOPSTICKS— KUAI-ZI— MEANS "QUICK LITTLE FELLOWS."

In Japan, you can buy a portable cooler on wheels for a watermelon.

The **cherimoya fruit,** native to **South America,** tastes like **bubble gum.**

CHILIES WERE USED TO CURE HEADACHES IN CHINA 2,000 YEARS AGO.

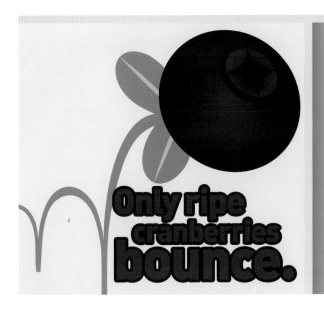

Only ripe cranberries **bounce.**

NORWAY FACED A NATIONWIDE **BUTTER** SHORTAGE IN 2011.

Happy New Year!

SPAIN: AT THE STROKE OF MIDNIGHT, EAT 12 GRAPES FOR GOOD LUCK.

MOBILE, ALABAMA, U.S.A.: SEE THE 12-FOOT (3.65 m) MECHANICAL MOON PIE DROP.

DILLSBURG, PENNSYLVANIA, U.S.A.: WATCH A 3-FOOT-TALL (1 m) LIGHT-UP PAPIER-MÂCHÉ PICKLE DROP FROM A FLAGPOLE.

LONDON, ENGLAND: ON NEW YEAR'S EVE 2013, BANANA-FLAVORED CONFETTI, PEACH-FLAVORED SNOWFLAKES, AND ORANGE-SCENTED BUBBLES FLOATED DOWN ON REVELERS.

GERMANY: EAT A GLÜCKSBRINGER, A **MARZIPAN PIG,** TO BRING GOOD LUCK!

AT BURGER KING IN JAPAN, YOU CAN BUY A "NINJA BURGER" —A HAMBURGER WITH HASH BROWNS AND A SLICE OF HAM ON A BLACK BUN.

THE **YARDLONG,**
AN ASIAN BEAN,
GROWS TO BE
NO MORE THAN
HALF A YARD (.46 m) **LONG.**

President Thomas Jefferson once received a 1,235-pound (560 kg) block of cheese as a gift.

AT A RESTAURANT IN NEW YORK,

WINNERS OF THE DAVEY JONES LOCKER CHALLENGE

EAT
2 POUNDS (9 kg) OF CRAB LEGS, **2 STUFFED** FISH FILLETS,

PLUS A **POUND** (.45 kg) **EACH** OF GRILLED JUMBO SHRIMP, STEAMED MUSSELS, AND FRIED CLAM STRIPS!

Ancient **forks** had only **2** prongs.

FANS OF THE
CHELSEA SOCCER CLUB
THROW CELERY
ON THE FIELD
TO TAUNT THE OPPOSING TEAM.

DURING THE 2013 HOLIDAY SEASON, PEOPLE IN **FINLAND** COULD PAY THEIR BUS FARES WITH GINGERBREAD COOKIES.

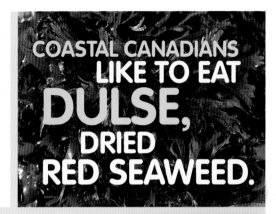

COASTAL CANADIANS **LIKE TO EAT DULSE,** DRIED **RED SEAWEED.**

ENGASTRATION=

cooking one food inside another food

IN PARTS OF FRANCE, **PIGS** ARE USED TO **SNIFF OUT** UNDERGROUND **TRUFFLES,** A TYPE OF EDIBLE FUNGUS.

THE MOST EXPENSIVE TRUFFLES CAN FETCH OVER $6,000 PER POUND!

DONUT + MUFFIN = DUFFIN

At the **Barbie Cafe** in Taipei, Taiwan, meals are served by waitstaff wearing **tiaras and pink tutus.**

A two-year-old **slice of cake** *served at the wedding of Britain's Prince William was recently auctioned for* **$4,160.**

DONUT + MUFFIN = DUFFIN

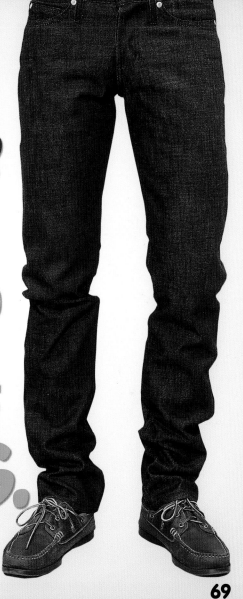

A CANADIAN **DESIGNER** RECENTLY CREATED MINT-SCENTED SCRATCH-AND-SNIFF *JEANS.*

THE WORLD'S **LARGEST PUMPKIN PIE** MEASURED **20 FEET** (6 m) ACROSS AND WEIGHED **3,699** (1,678 kg) **POUNDS!**

71

FOR $6,500, YOU CAN BUY A "CANDELIER," A LIGHT FIXTURE MADE OUT OF SOME **15,000** HAND-STRUNG **ACRYLIC GUMMY BEARS.**

Never cut your noodles in China: A long noodle represents a long life.

COOKED CARROTS ARE MORE NUTRITIOUS THAN RAW ONES.

IN A **SCOTTISH** HAGGIS-HURLING COMPETITION, PEOPLE STAND ON TOP OF BARRELS AND THROW THE PUDDING UP TO **217** FEET. (66 m)

FREAKIES, QUISP, and KABOOM

were all breakfast cereals in the 1970s.

A PHILADELPHIA, PENNSYLVANIA, U.S.A.,

PHOTOGRAPHER
ARRANGES MEAT
INTO OBJECTS,
PEOPLE, AND PLACES—
LIKE THE UNITED STATES OF AMERICA.

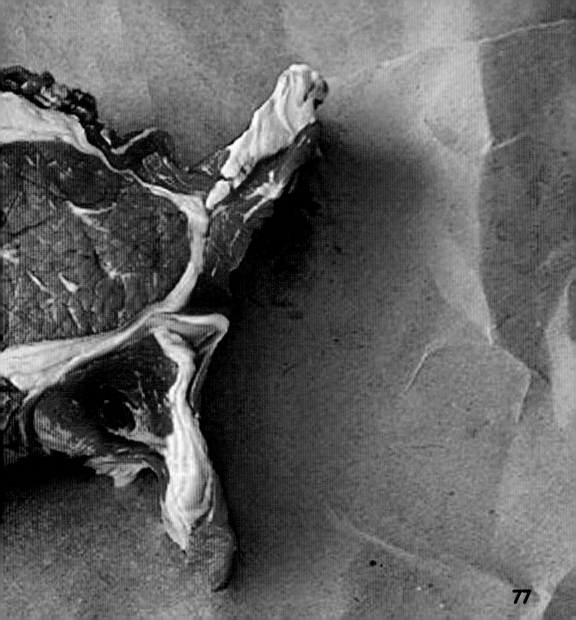

EVERY YEAR, MORE THAN **8 BILLION SWEETHEARTS** CANDY CONVERSATION HEARTS ARE MADE— ENOUGH LOVE TO GIVE ONE TO EVERY PERSON IN THE WORLD!

MARCHERS IN THE ANNUAL **CHRISTMAS PARADE** IN BERRIEN SPRINGS, MICHIGAN, U.S.A., **THROW PICKLES TO SPECTATORS.**

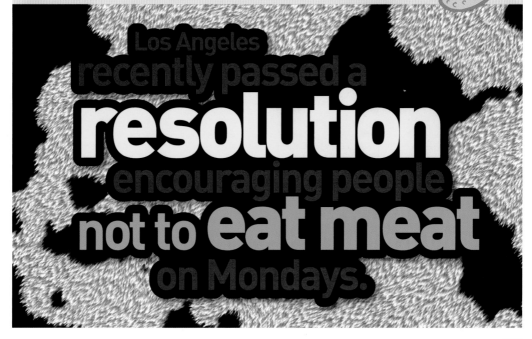

Los Angeles recently passed a **resolution** encouraging people **not to eat meat** on Mondays.

RESEARCHERS FOUND PIECES OF **5,500-YEAR-OLD BREAD** IN A PIT IN OXFORDSHIRE, ENGLAND.

You have to have a prescription to buy gum in Singapore.

In the 1830s, ketchup was sold in pill form as a treatment for stomach ailments.

THE **WORD** USED TO DESCRIBE THE **COLOR ORANGE** CAME ALONG AFTER THE FRUIT WAS NAMED **"ORANGE."**

More than one-third of all **pizzas** in America are covered with **pepperoni**, the most popular **topping** in the country.

ALEKTOROPHOBIA: fear of chicken

Beverages SERVED IN A **blue glass** SEEM **colder** THAN ONES SERVED IN A **red** or **green glass,** A STUDY FOUND.

Laetiporus mushrooms taste like chicken.

In southern **Africa,** people catch, squish, dry, and eat giant **caterpillars** called **mopane worms.**

Invented more than 1,000 years ago, **caramel** was first used to remove body hair.

THERE ARE ABOUT **7,000 CHERRIES** ON THE AVERAGE **TART CHERRY TREE.**

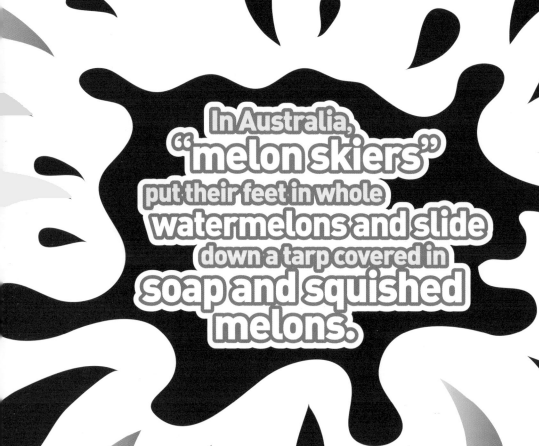

In Australia, "melon skiers" put their feet in whole watermelons and slide down a tarp covered in soap and squished melons.

KENTUCKY FRIED CHICKEN

IS A POPULAR CHRISTMAS EVE DINNER IN JAPAN.

IT DOESN'T MATTER WHAT COLOR FROOT LOOPS YOU EAT; THEY ARE ALL THE SAME FLAVOR.

The world's **largest chicken nugget** weighed **52 pounds.** (23.6 kg) That's **720 times** the size of a normal **nugget!**

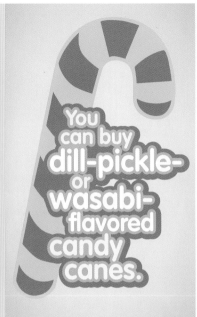

You can buy dill-pickle- or wasabi- flavored candy canes.

RADISHES WERE USED TO EMBALM THE DEAD IN ANCIENT EGYPT.

Scientists are working on inventing a plate that doesn't need to be washed.

THE COLOR OF THE TWIST TIES ON BREAD LOAVES IS CODE FOR THE DAY OF THE WEEK **THE BREAD WAS BAKED.**

BARBECUING **IN THE STREET IS A FORM OF PROTEST** IN BRAZIL.

A gadget that attaches to a **smartphone** can emit **scents** of different foods—like **sizzling meat.**

AT A **RESTAURANT** IN THE MALDIVE ISLANDS, **THE DINING ROOM IS UNDERWATER, 16 FEET BELOW SEA LEVEL.**

(5 m)

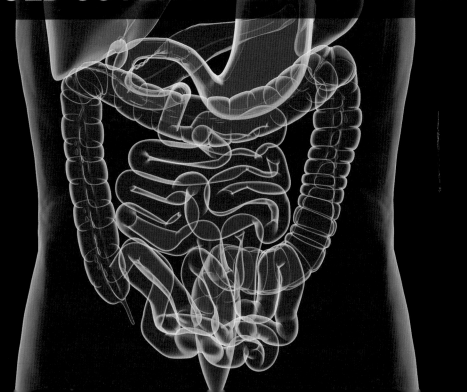

THE TOTAL SURFACE AREA OF YOUR **SMALL INTESTINE—AN ORGAN THAT HELPS DIGEST YOUR FOOD—** COULD COVER A **TENNIS COURT.**

It takes about **36 apples** to make a (3.79 L) gallon of **apple cider.**

Pets Deli in Berlin, Germany, serves *gourmet meals* for *dogs and cats.*

The ice crystals in **Dippin' Dots** are 50 times smaller than the ones in regular ice cream.

HARD-BOILING A CHICKEN **EGG** TAKES ABOUT

12 MINUTES.

HARD-BOILING AN OSTRICH **EGG?** ABOUT

90 MINUTES.

ON THE INTERNATIONAL SPACE STATION, BOWLS AND DISHES ARE VELCROED TO THE TABLE TO KEEP THEM FROM FLOATING AWAY.

The **stinky** aromas of blue cheese and sweaty feet are caused by the same **bacteria.**

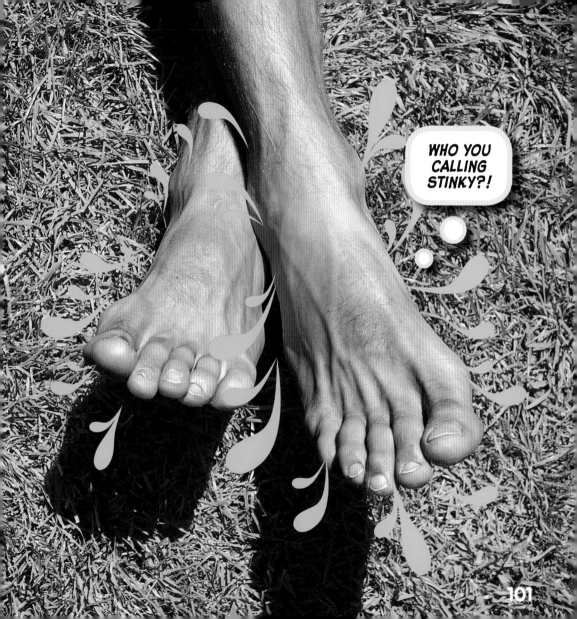

101

CHEERIOS WERE
ORIGINALLY CALLED

CHEERI OATS.

A PHILADELPHIA, PENNSYLVANIA, U.S.A., **RESTAURANT**

MAKES
TACO SHELLS OUT OF
BACON.

A **survey** *of nearly* **3,000 people** *in Britain revealed that the* **#1 breakfast annoyance** *is* **spreading butter** *that is too cold.*

GOODUCKEN=
A CHICKEN INSIDE
A DUCK INSIDE A GOOSE

Using jellyfish proteins, a man invented a type of **ice cream that glows** after you lick it.

ADDING **BACTERIA** TO CANDY MAY ONE DAY HELP PREVENT CAVITIES.

YOU CAN MAKE JEWELRY FROM **DEHYDRATED POTATOES.**

400 years ago, English women decorated their hats and dresses with **carrot leaves.**

The West African **"miracle berry"** tricks your taste buds into thinking **sour** food is **sweet.**

A **YAM** IS MORE CLOSELY RELATED TO A **LILY** THAN TO A **SWEET POTATO.**

The peak time for **passing gas** is five hours after you've had lunch or dinner.

IN THE 19TH CENTURY, **WARRIORS** IN KIRIBATI, AN ISLAND NATION IN **THE PACIFIC,** WORE ARMOR MADE OF COCONUTS AND FISH.

SPAM-FLAVORED POPSICLES ARE SOLD IN HAWAII.

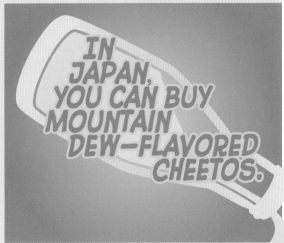

IN JAPAN, YOU CAN BUY MOUNTAIN DEW—FLAVORED CHEETOS.

A **LEMON TREE** CAN PRODUCE UP TO **600 POUNDS** OF FRUIT A (272 kg) YEAR—THAT'S ENOUGH TO MAKE 100 PITCHERS OF **LEMONADE!**

The co-inventor of the cotton candy machine was a dentist.

A **HAMBURGER** MADE FROM MEAT GROWN IN A SCIENCE LAB COST **$325,000—** ABOUT **100,000 TIMES** THE PRICE OF A REGULAR BURGER.

To promote the newly invented **Dubble Bubble gum,** salesmen for the Fleer Company taught people how to **blow bubbles.**

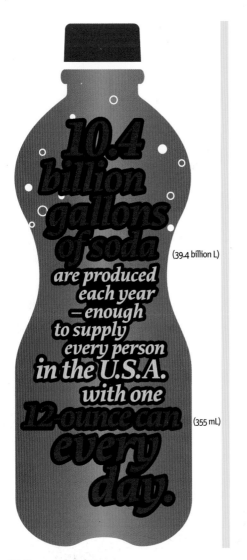

10.4 billion gallons of soda (39.4 billion L) *are produced each year — enough to supply every person in the U.S.A. with one 12-ounce can* (355 mL) *every day.*

The average Italian consumes half a pound of bread (.23 kg) **a day.**

RICH DARK

THE LARGEST **HERSHEY'S KISS** EVER MADE **WEIGHED 30,540 POUNDS—** (13,853 kg) THAT'S AS MUCH AS ALMOST **3 MILLION** REGULAR KISSES!

A PASTRY CHEF ONCE MADE A **300-POUND** (136 kg) REPLICA OF THE **WHITE HOUSE OUT OF GINGERBREAD.**

NEW ENGLANDERS EAT FIDDLEHEADS, CURLED-UP FRONDS OF BABY FERNS.

TUDOR CHRISTMAS PIE=
A PIGEON INSIDE
A PARTRIDGE
INSIDE A CHICKEN
INSIDE A GOOSE
INSIDE A TURKEY
INSIDE A PIE CRUST

THE AVERAGE AMERICAN KID WILL EAT 1,500 **PEANUT BUTTER AND JELLY** SANDWICHES BEFORE GRADUATING FROM HIGH SCHOOL.

A BRITISH MAN SET A WORLD RECORD BY **THROWING A PEANUT 124 FEET—** (38 m) ABOUT THE LENGTH OF 3½ SCHOOL BUSES.

Baskin-Robbins once made **ketchup-flavored** ice cream.

TUROPHOBIA: FEAR OF CHEESE

Deep-fried **tarantulas** are popular snacks in Cambodia.

115

THE MARSHMALLOWS IN LUCKY CHARMS CEREAL ARE CALLED "MARBITS."

IT TAKES ABOUT
350 SQUIRTS
FROM A
COW'S UDDER
TO MAKE ONE GALLON OF MILK.
(3.8 L)

KNIFE + FORK = KNORK

SPOON + KNIFE = SPIFE

SPOON + FORK = SPORK

The world's biggest chocolate bar weighed 12,770 pounds— about the same as an African elephant.

(5,792 kg)

THE AVERAGE **AMERICAN EATS** ABOUT **4,500** CALORIES ON THANKSGIVING— THAT'S THE SAME AS EATING 26 SLICES OF CHEESE PIZZA!

Food neophobia: fear of trying new foods

It's harder to taste sweet and salty foods while flying in an airplane.

A CALIFORNIA MAN SET A WORLD RECORD BY EATING 69 HOT DOGS IN 10 MINUTES.

A STUDY FOUND THAT IT WOULD TAKE **2.4 MILLION SEAGULLS** TO LIFT THE PEACH IN JAMES AND THE GIANT PEACH— **NOT 501**, AS THE BOOK SAYS.

CERTAIN KINDS OF BALSAMIC VINEGAR COST MORE THAN $60 AN OUNCE. (29.6 mL)

Workers at an ice cream shop in California, U.S.A., churn ice cream using bicycles.

THE **CHANDELIER** IN THE **COCONUT PALACE**
IN THE PHILIPPINES IS MADE OF
101 **COCONUT SHELLS!**

A **CAFE** IN JAPAN OFFERS SOLO CUSTOMERS A **GIANT STUFFED ANIMAL** TO KEEP THEM COMPANY AS THEY **EAT.**

TO PROMOTE ITS PRODUCT, A BRITISH COOKIE COMPANY ONCE INSTALLED LICKABLE WALLPAPER IN AN ELEVATOR IN LONDON.

"COCA-COLA" IS THE SECOND MOST UNDERSTOOD WORD IN THE WORLD, AFTER "OK."

THE AVERAGE AMERICAN SPENDS 1.25 HOURS PER DAY EATING AND DRINKING.

ABOUT 2 MILLION
JUMBO TURKEY LEGS
ARE SOLD ANNUALLY
AT U.S. DISNEY
THEME PARKS.

IN JAPAN, THE McDONALD'S "CHERRY BLOSSOM BURGER" HAS A PINK BUN.

127

Cloud ears are a type of mushroom used in Chinese cooking.

A man in Israel grew a **lemon** the size of a **basketball!**

THE **MYSTERY FLAVORS** OF **DUM DUM LOLLIPOPS** ARE TWO REGULAR FLAVORS **MIXED TOGETHER.**
(THEY ARE CREATED WHEN ONE FLAVOR ENDS ON THE PRODUCTION LINE AND THE NEXT FLAVOR STARTS.)

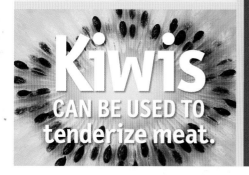

Kiwis CAN BE USED TO tenderize meat.

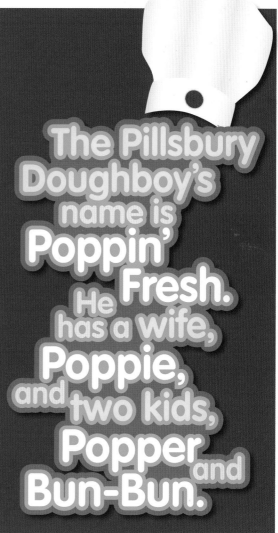

The Pillsbury Doughboy's name is **Poppin' Fresh.** He has a wife, **Poppie,** and **two kids, Popper** and **Bun-Bun.**

For **one year,** a Seattle, Washington, U.S.A., **woman** ate every meal at a **coffee shop.**

Some coffee shops pump artificial coffee scents into the air to entice customers.

15 MILLION SNICKERS BARS ARE PRODUCED EVERY DAY. THAT'S NEARLY ENOUGH TO GIVE EVERY PERSON IN NEW YORK CITY TWO BARS!

Red is the most popular color of **gummy candy.**

UNTIL 500 YEARS AGO, NO ONE OUTSIDE NORTH AND SOUTH **AMERICA** HAD EVER TASTED CHILI PEPPERS, CHOCOLATE, OR **TOMATOES.**

IN A RECENT STUDY, **54%** OF THE PEOPLE POLLED ADMITTED TO SERVING FOOD AFTER IT FELL ON THE FLOOR.

Scientists recently found **bits of a date** stuck in the teeth of a 40,000-year-old Neanderthal.

THE RESTAURANT CREDITED WITH INVENTING THE HAMBURGER HAS A STRICT "NO KETCHUP" RULE.

One copy of *Modernist Cuisine,* the world's most expensive cookbook, costs **$625.**

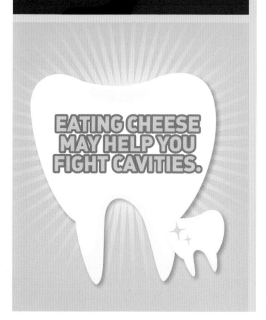

EATING CHEESE MAY HELP YOU FIGHT CAVITIES.

AT A *CHICAGO WHITE SOX BASE-BALL GAME,* YOU CAN ORDER A *"WALKING TACO"* —A BAG OF FRITOS WITH NACHO CHEESE AND CHILI POURED INTO IT.

EACH
BLUE STICKER
ON A CHIQUITA
BANANA IS
PLACED THERE
BY HAND.

AN AVOCADO HAS MORE

MOST BANANAS ARE GENETICALLY IDENTICAL.

THAN TWICE AS MUCH POTASSIUM AS A BANANA.

AN 18-INCH-LONG (46 CM)

CORN DOG

VEGETATE ARIZONA BALLPARK IS ROUGHLY EQUIVALENT TO

9 PEANUT BUTTER SANDWICHES.

Coconut water has been used as a short-term substitute for human blood plasma.

You can buy smoked-salmon gelato in Rome, Italy.

Canada has more donut shops per person than any other country.

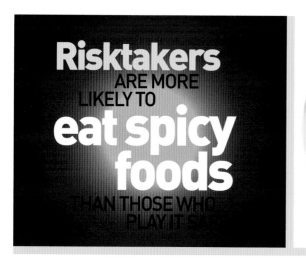

Risktakers ARE MORE LIKELY TO **eat spicy foods** THAN THOSE WHO PLAY IT SAFE

Baconnaise, bacon-flavored mayonnaise, doesn't contain any **bacon.**

THE WORD *RAMBUTAN*— **THE NAME OF A FRUIT NATIVE TO ASIA—MEANS "HAIRY" IN MALAYSIAN.**

IN WISCONSIN, CHEESE BRINE HAS BEEN USED TO THAW ICY ROADS.

IT WOULD TAKE RUNNING A MARATHON TO BURN OFF ALL THE CALORIES IN TWO FAST-FOOD MEALS.

ON THE INTERNATIONAL SPACE STATION, **93 PERCENT** OF THE **ASTRONAUTS' SWEAT AND URINE** IS RECYCLED INTO **DRINKING WATER.**

143

A BAKERY IN THE U.K. CREATED AN

8-TIER WEDDING CAKE COVERED WITH 2,000 DIAMONDS—WORTH ABOUT $50 MILLION.

THE WORLD RECORD FOR **EATING** A MEDIUM-SIZE **PIZZA** IS 41 SECONDS.

IN SINGAPORE, YOU CAN BUY HOT MASHED POTATOES OUT OF A VENDING MACHINE.

VISITORS CAN MAKE THEIR OWN **"FRESH" NOODLE SOUP** AT THE MOMOFUKU ANDO INSTANT RAMEN MUSEUM IN OSAKA, JAPAN.

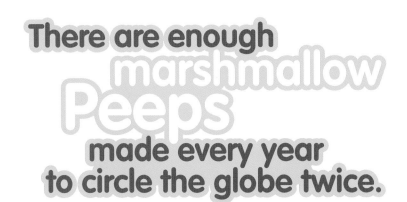

There are enough marshmallow Peeps made every year to circle the globe twice.

THE WORLD'S **LOUDEST** RECORDED **BURP** WAS LOUDER THAN A HAND DRILL.

Almost 4,000 years ago, ancient Chinese people buried hunks of cheese with the dead.

The world's **longest carrot** grew as long as **an SUV.**

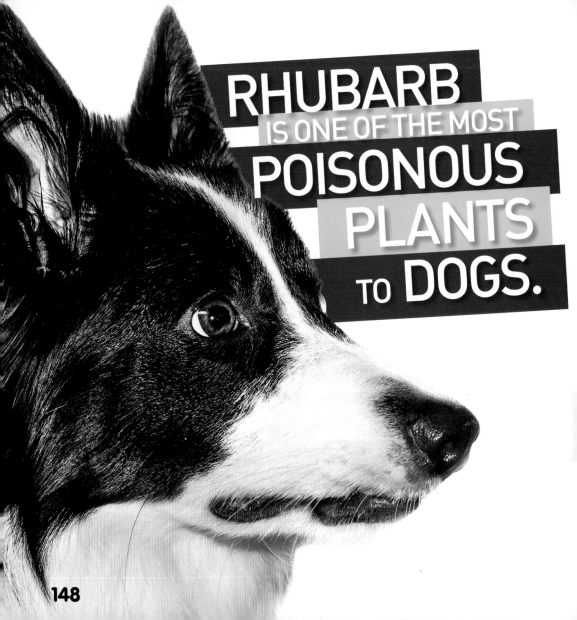

RHUBARB IS ONE OF THE MOST POISONOUS PLANTS TO DOGS.

A New Jersey, U.S.A., museum is home to a collection of over 5,400 spoons!

The color red can make you feel hungry.

Enough **jelly beans** are made each spring to fill a plastic **Easter egg** as tall as a **nine-story building.**

Miners traded gold for potatoes during the California gold rush.

THE WAIT LIST TO EAT AT A RESTAURANT IN EARLTON, NEW YORK, U.S.A., **IS 10 YEARS LONG.**

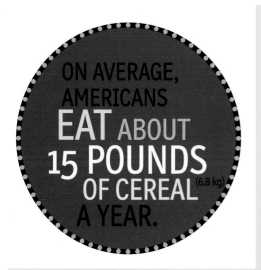

ON AVERAGE, AMERICANS **EAT** ABOUT **15 POUNDS** OF CEREAL (6.8 kg) A YEAR.

A MAN ONCE **ATE** 233 RAW **OYSTERS** IN THREE MINUTES.

Ancient Greeks believed **mint** could cure hiccups.

An Oreo vending machine once dispensed **3-D printed** cookies to customers.

BRUSSELS SPROUTS + **KALE**

BRUSSELS KALE

AN **ISRAELI ARTIST** CREATES MINIATURE
REPLICAS OF FOOD
THAT ARE **12 TIMES** SMALLER
THAN THE REAL THING.

In the U.K., **waffle fries** can be made in **social media shapes,** like **hashtags,** **emoticons,** and **@ signs.**

U.S. ARMY SCIENTISTS INVENTED A PIZZA THAT CAN BE STORED AT ROOM TEMPERATURE FOR THREE YEARS WITHOUT GOING BAD.

KIDS WHO LIKE SWEET FOODS BETTER THAN SALTY ONES TEND TO BE TALLER FOR THEIR AGE.

Mangoes are related to pistachios— and **poison ivy.**

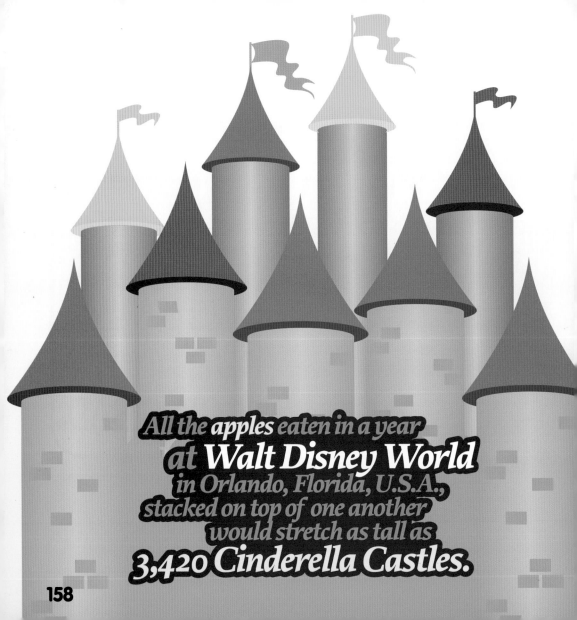

All the *apples* eaten in a year at **Walt Disney World** in Orlando, Florida, U.S.A., stacked on top of one another would stretch as tall as **3,420 Cinderella Castles.**

A **JAPANESE DESIGNER** CREATES EDIBLE PLATES, BOWLS, AND CHOPSTICKS USING A SPECIAL KIND OF BISCUIT DOUGH.

TWO FOOD ARTISTS MADE A REPLICA OF THE LOUVRE'S FAMOUS PYRAMIDS USING GINGERBREAD, HARD CANDY, AND LICORICE.

TO GET PERFECTLY EVEN SLICES OF PIZZA, YOU CAN BUY A LASER-GUIDED CUTTER.

A restaurant **in New Zealand** shoots burgers to customers' tables **through** clear tubes at 87 miles an hour. (140 km/h)

The potato chip was invented in 1853 by George Crum.

25 PERCENT OF ALL GIRL SCOUT COOKIES SALES ARE THIN MINTS.

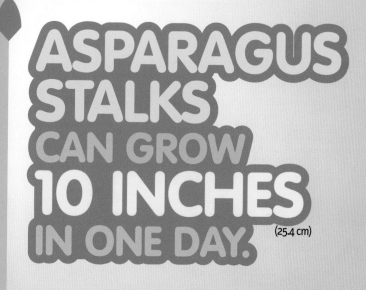

ASPARAGUS STALKS CAN GROW **10 INCHES** IN ONE DAY. (25.4 cm)

16TH-CENTURY
ITALIAN PAINTER
GIUSEPPE ARCIMBOLDO
PAINTED FRUITS AND
VEGETABLES
TO LOOK LIKE
HUMAN FACES.

IN COLONIAL AMERICA, FRUIT SELLERS RENTED PINEAPPLES TO USE AS CENTERPIECES.

You can buy a candle that smells like a hamburger.

In ancient Egypt, baskets of onions were given as funeral offerings.

MOST AMERICANS REGULARLY EAT FEWER THAN 30 DIFFERENT FOODS.

SWEET POTATOES
COME NOT ONLY IN
ORANGE,
BUT ALSO IN
WHITE,
YELLOW, RED,
AND PURPLE.

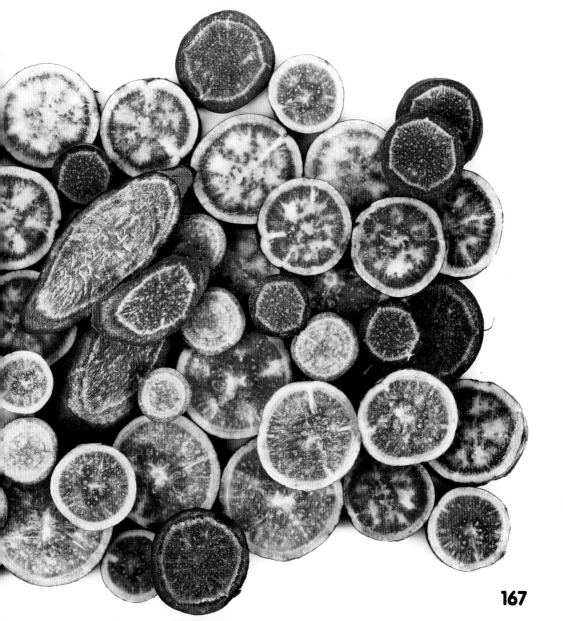

CHRISTOPHER COLUMBUS BROUGHT PICKLES WITH HIM ON HIS VOYAGE TO THE NEW WORLD.

YOU MIGHT NEED A TOOTHPICK TO GET RID OF A TOOTHPACK, THE FOOD THAT GETS STUCK IN YOUR MOLARS.

CHOCOLATE-COVERED BACON ON A STICK IS A POPULAR TREAT AT THE WISCONSIN, U.S.A., STATE FAIR.

CHERRY BLOSSOM, SWEET POTATO, AND BLACK SESAME SEED ARE ALL POPULAR ICE CREAM FLAVORS IN JAPAN.

The world's heaviest tomato weighed 7 pounds, 12 ounces—the same (3.51 kg) weight as a healthy newborn baby!

SLICED BREAD WAS ONCE BRIEFLY BANNED IN THE U.S.A.

A **BAKERY IN** **NEW YORK CITY** SOLD PUMPKIN DONUTS WITH TURKEY AND GRAVY FILLING DURING THANKSGIVING SEASON.

75,000 crocus flowers are needed to harvest just **one pound** of (.45 kg) **saffron,** the world's most expensive **spice.**

DINERS AT THE **ROBOT RESTAURANT** IN CHINA HAVE THEIR WHOLE MEAL **COOKED AND SERVED BY ROBOTS.**

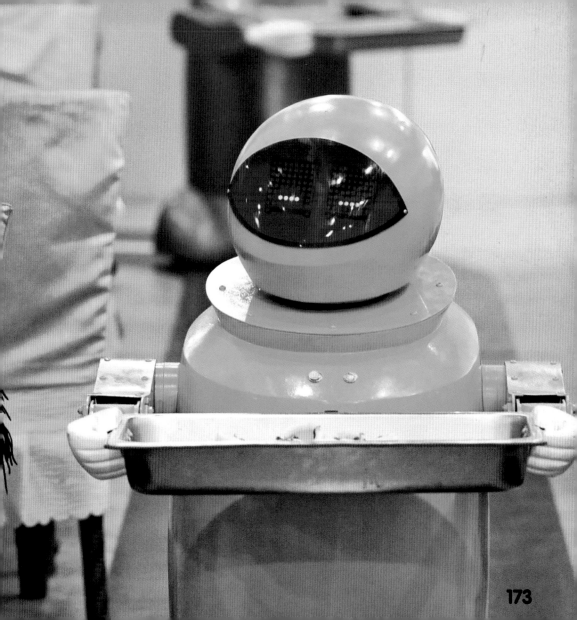

You can eat deep-fried *orchids* in *Thailand.*

Some **strawberries** weigh more than **two sticks of butter.**

CHOPSTICKS WERE INVENTED

SNAP, *CRACKLE*, POP (U.S.A.)

KNISPER, *KNASPER*, KNUSPER (GERMANY)

PIM, *PUM*, PAM (MEXICO)

PIF, *PAF*, POF (BELGIUM)

MORE THAN 4,000 YEARS AGO.

PEOPLE USED TO BELIEVE EATING PUMPKIN COULD REMOVE FRECKLES.

ONE OUT OF FIVE AMERICANS HAS EATEN AN ENTIRE PIE BY THEMSELVES.

THE WORLD'S **LARGEST GINGERBREAD VILLAGE** REQUIRED **2,240 POUNDS** (1,016 kg) OF **ICING,** **400 POUNDS** (181 kg) OF **CANDY,** AND **500 POUNDS** (227 kg) OF **DOUGH.**

EEL-FLAVORED SODA IS POPULAR IN JAPAN.

AT ONE LONDON CAFE, FOOD AND DRINKS ARE FREE, BUT YOU ARE CHARGED 5 CENTS FOR EVERY MINUTE YOU SIT.

YOU TYPICALLY SWALLOW AROUND 250 TIMES DURING A MEAL.

SOME RASPBERRIES ARE PURPLE!

YOU CAN'T MAKE FRENCH FRIES IN SPACE.

ALMOST HALF OF A MOVIE THEATER'S PROFITS ARE MADE FROM SELLING SNACKS.

MILLIONS OF YEARS AGO, GIANT GROUND SLOTHS ATE AVOCADOS.

Jackfruit— the largest fruit to grow on a tree—can weigh more than four watermelons.

COMPETITORS AT THE WORLD **PEA SHOOTING CHAMPIONSHIPS** IN ENGLAND BLAST PEAS *THROUGH BLOWPIPES* AT TARGETS.

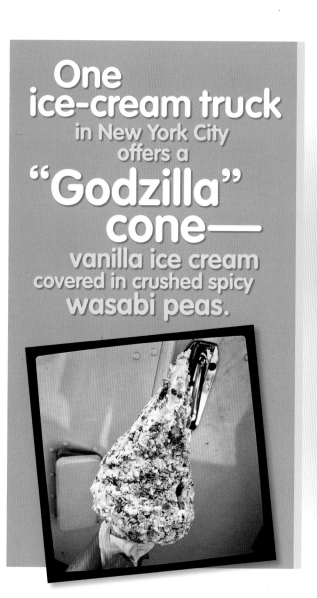

One ice-cream truck in New York City offers a **"Godzilla" cone**— vanilla ice cream covered in crushed spicy wasabi peas.

SOME PEOPLE **SHAMPOO** THEIR HAIR WITH **EGG YOLKS.**

SOME BANANAS HAVE

RED SKINS WITH **PINK FLESH—**

YET TASTE THE SAME AS THE YELLOW KIND.

73% of home cooks admit to licking the spoon.

A restaurant in Budapest, Hungary, offers nearly 2,000 items on its menu.

A company in England will **print** your photos on marshmallows.

You can order
a "milkshake burger"
——a cheeseburger topped
with deep-fried ice cream——
in Florida, U.S.A.

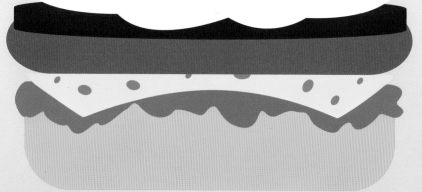

Macaroni and Cheese,

Asparagus,

and Cotton Candy

are not only foods;

they're also crayon colors.

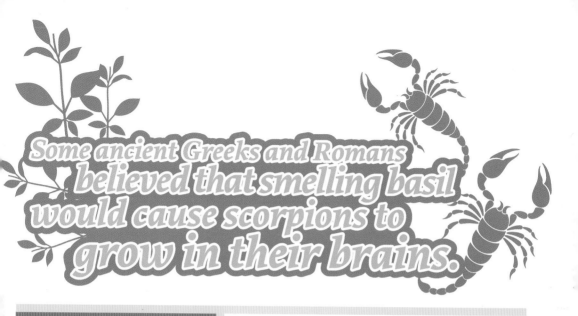

Some ancient Greeks and Romans believed that smelling basil would cause scorpions to grow in their brains.

Ancient Egyptians **ate** ham and eggs for **breakfast** more than **3,000** years ago.

A can of jellied cranberry sauce contains about **200** cranberries.

The Japanese tradition of **eating pufferfish**—one of the world's most poisonous fish— **kills five people** every year.

191

EARLY MOVIE THEATERS BANNED POPCORN BECAUSE IT WAS TOO MESSY.

U.S. PRESIDENT THOMAS JEFFERSON SERVED MACARONI AND CHEESE AT A STATE DINNER.

A diner in Ohio, U.S.A., serves **grilled cheese** sandwiches made with **DONUTS.**

DURING WORLD WAR II, KIDS WERE OFFERED **CARROTS-ON-A-STICK** INSTEAD OF ICE CREAM.

COFFEE BEANS ARE NOT TRUE BEANS. THEY'RE BERRY PITS.

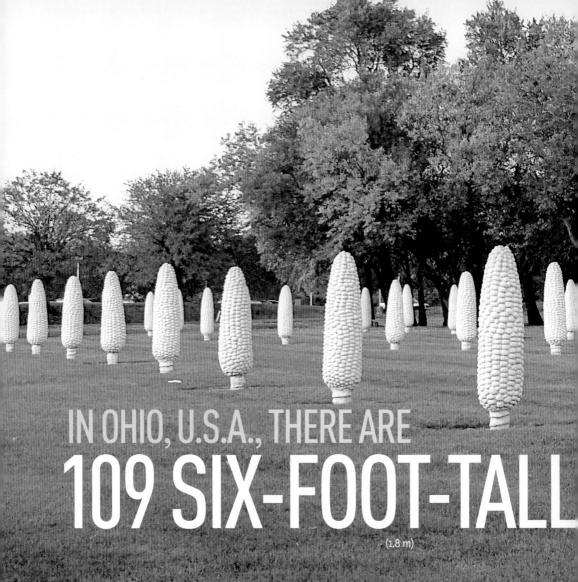

IN OHIO, U.S.A., THERE ARE
109 SIX-FOOT-TALL

(1.8 m)

196

CONCRETE EARS OF CORN

STANDING IN ROWS IN A FORMER CORNFIELD.

197

THAT'S WEIRD!

The world's heaviest **watermelon** weighed as much as **10 koalas!**

A GERMAN DESIGN COMPANY **MADE A COOKBOOK** ENTIRELY OUT OF **FRESH PASTA,** SO YOU CAN **READ IT, COOK IT, AND *EAT IT.***

FACTFINDER

Illustrations are indicated by
boldface.

200

FACT**FINDER**

FACT**FINDER**

Staff for This Book
Amy Briggs, *Project Manager*
Rebecca Baines, *Project Editor*
Julide Obuz Dengel, *Art Director*
Hillary Leo, *Photo Editor*
Rachael Hamm Plett, Moduza Design, *Designer*
Paige Towler, *Editorial Assistant*
Julie Beer and Sarah Wassner, *Researchers*
Allie Allen and Sanjida Rashid, *Design Production Assistants*
Michael Cassady, *Photo Assistant*
Michael Libonati, *Special Projects Assistant*
Grace Hill, *Associate Managing Editor*
Mike O'Connor, *Production Editor*
Lewis R. Bassford, *Production Manager*
Nicole Elliott, *Director of Production*
Susan Borke, *Legal and Business Affairs*

Published by the National Geographic Society
Gary E. Knell, *President and CEO*
John M. Fahey, *Chairman of the Board*
Melina Gerosa Bellows, *Chief Education Officer*
Declan Moore, *Chief Media Officer*
Hector Sierra, *Senior Vice President and General Manager, Book Division*

Senior Management Team, Kids Publishing and Media
Nancy Laties Feresten, *Senior Vice President;* Jennifer Emmett, *Vice President, Editorial Director, Kids Books;* Julie Vosburgh Agnone, *Vice President, Editorial Operations;* Rachel Buchholz, *Editor and Vice President,* NG Kids *magazine;* Michelle Sullivan, *Vice President, Kids Digital;* Eva Absher-Schantz, *Design Director;* Jay Sumner, *Photo Director;* Hannah August, *Marketing Director;* R. Gary Colbert, *Production Director*

Digital Anne McCormack, *Director;* Laura Goertzel, Sara Zeglin, *Producers;* Jed Winer, *Special Projects Assistant;* Emma Rigney, *Creative Producer;* Brian Ford, *Video Producer;* Bianca Bowman, *Assistant Producer;* Natalie Jones, *Senior Product Manager*

Based on the "Weird But True" department in *National Geographic Kids* magazine

PLAY with your FOOD!

See what **WEIRD, FUN,** and **YUMMY** treats you can create with this awesome cookbook, especially for YOU!

AVAILABLE WHEREVER BOOKS ARE SOLD
Discover more at kids.nationalgeographic.com

NATIONAL GEOGRAPHIC KiDS